This book belongs to:

.... Tessa Miller ....

From:

.... Youth Group ....

Date:

.... 9/5/21 ....

Originally published by iCharacter Ltd.
under the title *JOY Prayer Journal*

Copyright © 2018 by iCharacter Ltd. (Ireland)
www.iCharacter.org

Written by Agnes and Salem de Bezenac
Illustrated by Agnes de Bezenac

Published by arrangement with iCharacter Limited (Ireland)
by Christian Art Publishers,
PO Box 1599, Vereeniging, 1930, RSA

© 2019
First edition 2019

Cover designed by Christian Art Publishers

Printed in China

ISBN 978-1-4321-3081-7

19 20 21 22 23 24 25 26 27 28 – 10 9 8 7 6 5 4 3 2 1

MY Prayer JOURNAL

CHRISTIAN ART PUBLISHERS

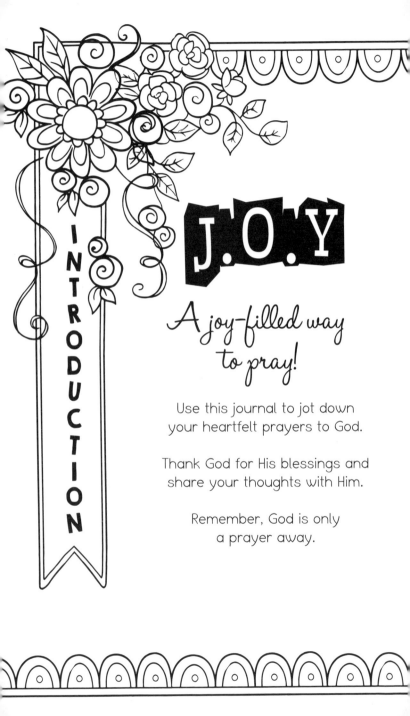

J.O.Y

A joy-filled way to pray!

INTRODUCTION

Use this journal to jot down your heartfelt prayers to God.

Thank God for His blessings and share your thoughts with Him.

Remember, God is only a prayer away.

Jesus
Others
You
spells JOY!

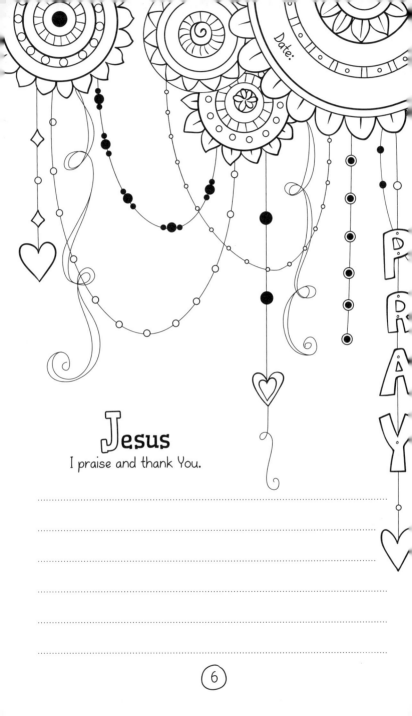

PRAY

Jesus
I praise and thank You.

....

....

....

....

....

....

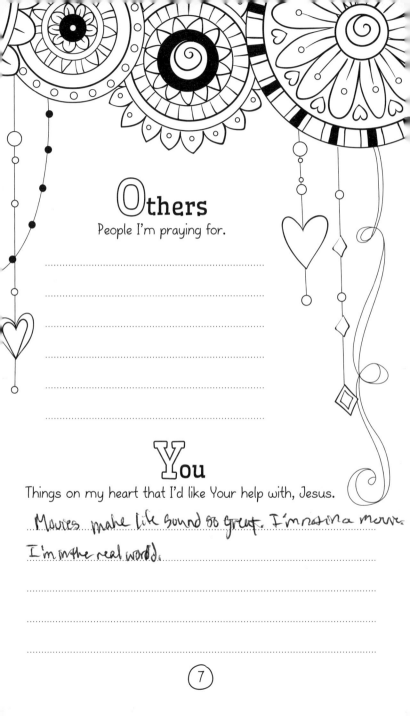

Others

People I'm praying for.

....
....
....
....
....
....

You

Things on my heart that I'd like Your help with, Jesus.

Movies make life sound so great. I'm not in a movie.
I'm in the real world.

....
....
....

Date:

Jesus
I praise and thank You.

....

....

....

....

....

....

....

....

Others

People I'm praying for.

....

....

....

....

....

You

Things on my heart that I'd like Your help with, Jesus.

....

....

....

....

Jesus

I praise and thank You.

....

....

....

....

....

....

....

....

....

....

....

....

Others
People I'm praying for.

....

....

....

....

You
Things on my heart that I'd like Your help with, Jesus.

....

....

....

....

....

....

Date:

Date:

Jesus

I praise and thank You.

....

....

....

....

....

....

....

Others
People I'm praying for.

....

....

....

....

....

You
Things on my heart that I'd like Your help with, Jesus.

....

....

....

....

....

Date:

Jesus
I praise and thank You.

....

....

....

....

....

....

....

....

A verse on prayer:

PRAY

Others
People I'm praying for.

....
....
....
....

You
Things on my heart that I'd like Your help with, Jesus.

....
....
....
....

Jesus

I praise and thank You.

....
....
....
....
....
....
....
....
....

Date:

Others

People I'm praying for.

....

....

....

You

Things on my heart that I'd
like Your help with, Jesus.

....

....

....

....

....

....

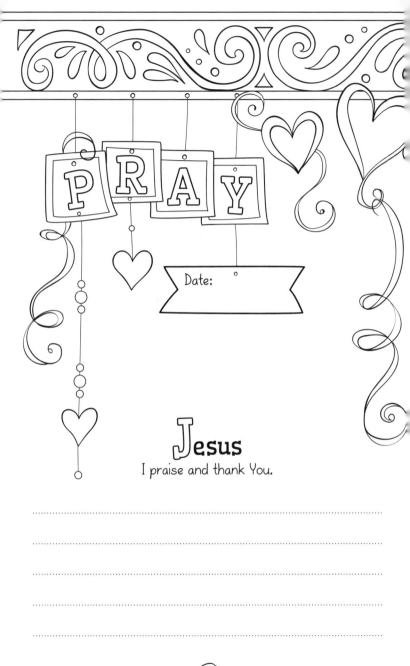

PRAY

Date:

Jesus
I praise and thank You.

....

....

....

....

....

Others

People I'm praying for.

....

....

....

....

....

....

You

Things on my heart that I'd like Your help with, Jesus.

....

....

....

....

....

Jesus

I praise and thank You.

Date:

Others
People I'm praying for.

....

....

....

....

....

You
Things on my heart that I'd like Your help with, Jesus.

....

....

....

....

....

....

....

....

....

PRAY

Date:

Jesus
I praise and thank You.

....

....

....

....

....

....

....

....

....

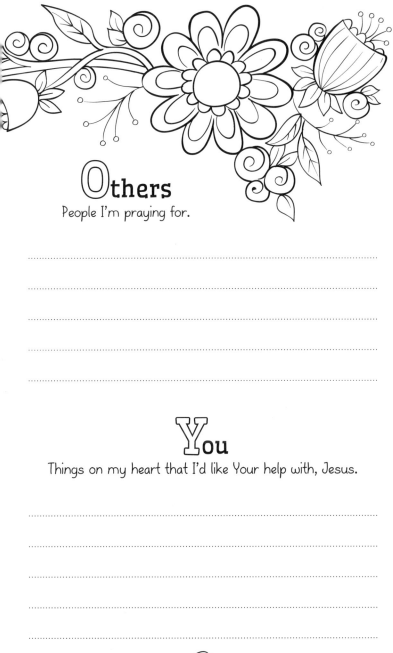

Others

People I'm praying for.

....

....

....

....

....

You

Things on my heart that I'd like Your help with, Jesus.

....

....

....

....

....

Jesus

I praise and thank You.

....

....

....

....

....

....

....

....

....

....

....

....

A verse on
prayer:

24

Others

People I'm praying for.

....

....

....

....

....

You

Things on my heart that I'd like Your help with, Jesus.

....

....

....

....

....

....

Date:

Date:

Jesus
I praise and thank You.

....
....
....
....
....
....
....
....

Others

People I'm praying for.

....

....

....

....

....

....

You

Things on my heart that I'd like Your help with, Jesus.

....

....

....

....

....

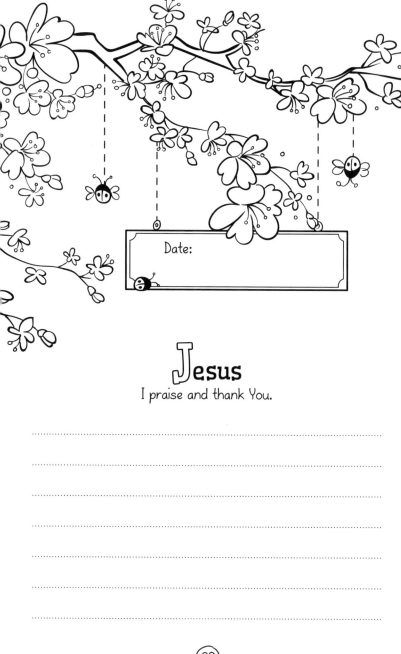

Date:

Jesus
I praise and thank You.

....

....

....

....

....

....

....

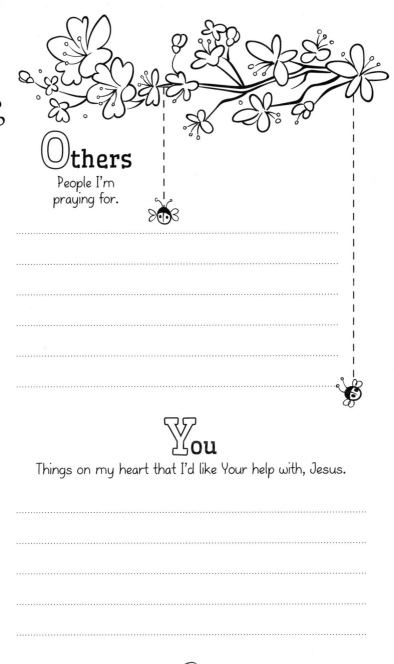

Others

People I'm
praying for.

....

....

....

....

....

....

You

Things on my heart that I'd like Your help with, Jesus.

....

....

....

....

....

Jesus

I praise and thank You.

Date:

Others

People I'm praying for.

....

....

....

....

You

Things on my heart that I'd like Your help with, Jesus.

....

....

....

....

Date:

Jesus
I praise and thank You.

Others

People I'm praying for.

....

....

....

....

....

You

Things on my heart that I'd like Your help with, Jesus.

....

....

....

....

....

Jesus

I praise and thank You.

....
....
....
....
....
....
....

Date:

Others
People I'm praying for.

....

....

....

....

....

You
Things on my heart that I'd
like Your help with, Jesus.

....

....

....

....

....

Date:

Jesus
I praise and thank You.

....

....

....

....

....

....

....

....

....

Others

People I'm praying for.

....

....

....

....

....

....

You

Things on my heart that I'd like Your help with, Jesus.

....

....

....

....

....

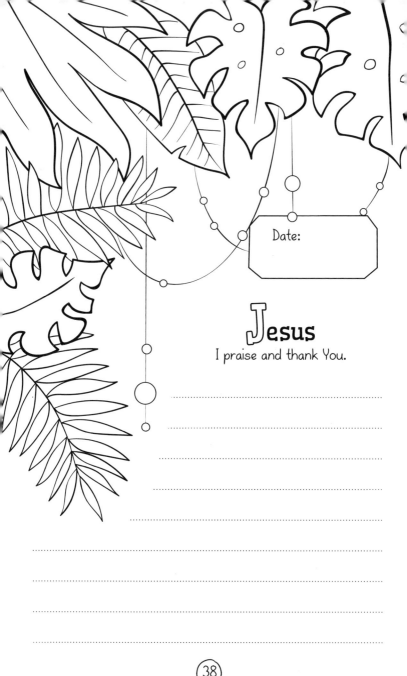

Date:

Jesus

I praise and thank You.

....
....
....
....
....
....
....
....

Others

People I'm praying for.

....

....

....

....

....

You

Things on my heart that I'd like Your help with, Jesus.

....

....

....

....

....

Jesus

I praise and thank You.

Date:

Others

People I'm praying for.

....

....

....

....

....

You

Things on my heart that I'd like Your help with, Jesus.

....

....

....

....

....

....

Date:

Jesus
I praise and thank You.

Others

People I'm praying for.

....

....

....

....

....

You

Things on my heart that I'd like Your help with, Jesus.

....

....

....

....

Jesus

I praise and thank You.

....

....

....

....

....

....

....

....

....

....

Date:

Others

People I'm praying for.

....

....

....

....

....

....

You

Things on my heart that I'd like Your help with, Jesus.

....

....

....

....

....

Date:

Jesus
I praise and thank You.

....

....

....

....

....

....

....

....

....

....

Others

People I'm praying for.

....

....

....

....

....

....

You

Things on my heart that I'd like Your help with, Jesus.

....

....

....

....

....

....

Jesus
I praise and thank You.

....

....

....

....

....

....

....

....

....

Date:

Others

People I'm praying for.

....

....

....

....

....

You

Things on my heart that I'd like Your help with, Jesus.

....

....

....

....

....

....

Jesus

I praise and thank You.

....

....

....

....

....

....

....

....

Date:

Others

People I'm praying for.

....

....

....

....

....

....

You

Things on my heart that I'd like Your help with, Jesus.

....

....

....

....

....

....

Jesus

I praise and thank You.

....
....
....
....

Date:

Others
People I'm praying for.

....

....

....

....

....

You
Things on my heart that I'd like Your help with, Jesus.

....

....

....

....

....

....

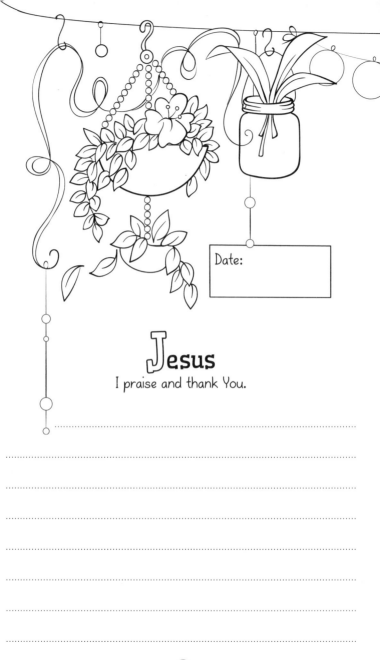

Date:

Jesus
I praise and thank You.

....

....

....

....

....

....

....

PRAY

Others
People I'm praying for.

....

....

....

....

....

....

You
Things on my heart that I'd like Your help with, Jesus.

....

....

....

....

....

Date:

Jesus
I praise and thank You.

....

....

....

....

....

....

....

....

pray

Others
People I'm praying for.

....
....
....
....
....
....

You
Things on my heart that I'd like Your help with, Jesus.

....
....
....
....
....

Jesus

I praise and thank You.

....

....

....

....

....

....

....

....

Date:

....

....

....

Others

People I'm praying for.

....

....

....

....

You

Things on my heart that I'd like Your help with, Jesus.

....

....

....

....

....

....

Date:

Jesus
I praise and thank You.

....
....
....
....
....
....
....
....

Others
People I'm praying for.

....
....
....
....
....
....

You
Things on my heart that I'd like Your help with, Jesus.

....
....
....
....
....

Date:

Jesus
I praise and thank You.

....

....

....

....

....

....

....

....

Others
People I'm praying for.

....

....

....

....

....

....

You
Things on my heart that I'd like Your help with, Jesus.

....

....

....

....

....

Agnes de Bezenac lives with her husband, Salem, and their two children in the countryside of France. Their love and devotion for children has led them to many a place and country, while gaining experience through media productions and educating children about life, good morals and biblical principles.
They have a deep love for God and enjoy sharing it with kids in simple ways that they can understand, through art and positive illustrations.